TIKI Drinks

TIKI

DRINKS

ADAM ROCKE

Illustrations by SHAG

SURREY BOOKS CHICAGO

To Tracey, Darla, and Veronica

TIKI DRINKS is published by Surrey Books,
230 E. Ohio St., Suite 120, Chicago, IL 60611.

Illustrations by Shag
Designed and typeset by Joan Sommers
 Design, Chicago
Printed and bound in China by
C&C Offset Printing Co., Ltd.

5 4

Library of Congress Cataloging-in-Publication Data

Rocke, Adam
   Tiki drinks / Adam Rocke ; illustrations by Shag
   p. cm.
   ISBN 1-57284-036-6
   1. Cocktails. 2. Bartending. I. Title
TX951.R65 2000
641.8'74--dc21

                        00-058774

For free book catalog and prices on quantity
purchases, contact Surrey Books at the
address above, or at www.surreybooks.com.

Distributed to the trade by
Publishers Group West.

Illustrations: *Banana Liquer*, 1998 (frontis-
piece); *Tutuila, Ofu, and Tau*, 1999 (pp.4–5);
Rum Demon, 1997 (p. 6); *The Salesman*, 1998
(p. 15); *Crandall Meets His Match*, 2000
(pp. 20–21); *The Peers*, 1999 (pp. 28–29);
The Madonna of Mai Kai, 2000 (pp. 34–35);
The Chemistry Lesson, 1998 (pp.42–43);
Headhunter, Man About Town, 1999
(pp. 48–49); *The Distraught Tiki*, 1999
(pp. 56–57).

Introduction

WITH EVERY SIP OF A TIKI DRINK, YOU SHOULD expect to be whisked away to a lush, tropical island surrounded by warm, turquoise waters. Gentle trade winds should continuously fill your nostrils with the delicate scents of palm oil and coconut. Scantily clad insignificant others with perfect bodies should attend to your every need as you lie in an oversized hammock, suspended between two towering palm trees.

OK, that's what you might expect. What you get might depend on your Tiki skills, and adding a repertory of fabulous Tiki drinks to your mixology arsenal will certainly improve your chances. They're much easier to make than you might think, and you'll probably draw a crowd—and much admiration—as you weave your Tiki magic at parties. Let's start with the basics.

First, you'll learn how to set up your very own Tiki bar—from the basic ingredients to the necessary mixing tools and utensils to the proper glassware for each drink. Next, I'll provide you with a table of measurements, just in case dash, shot, and jigger are terms alien to your liquor lingo. And finally, I'll give you a healthy dose of my favorite Tiki recipes, more than enough to cause you to hunger for cracked conch, mango salad, and grilled grouper.

So break out the sunblock, throw on your shades, don your favorite swimsuit, and sidle up to the bar.

It's Tiki time.

Setting up your Tiki bar

Utensils

When it comes to Tiki drinks, the most important item in your arsenal is the blender. I recommend a durable model (glass or stainless steel) with multiple speeds. Regardless of the model you choose, as long as it can reduce crushed ice to a smooth consistency, it will do the job.

Many of the other utensils required for setting up a standard bar can be used for your Tiki bar. They are:

Can and bottle openers

Corkscrew (the new air-powered "pump" varieties are excellent)

Cutting board (wooden or synthetic)

Ice bucket (with plenty of ice!)

Ice cream scoop

Ice tongs or scoop

Juicer (a.k.a juice extractor)

Knives (any small set; make sure a paring knife is included)

Lemon/lime squeezer

Measuring set (includes various-sized cups and spoons)

Miniature umbrellas (an absolute must!)

Mixing glass

Mixing stick (a.k.a muddler; usually wooden)

Napkins (cocktail and, for goblet-sized drinks, dinner)

Pitchers (for measuring and/or serving)

Plastic straws (cocktail and long)

Shaker set (consisting of a metal tumbler and a mixing glass)

Spoons (teaspoons and tablespoons, if not in measuring set)

Strainer (two: medium and very fine mesh)

Swizzle sticks

Toothpicks (for garnishes)

Towels or rags (for cleaning purposes)

Glasses

Scorpion bowls, tiki volcanoes, and Buddha-shaped goblets are great if you want to go all out. Otherwise, here's what I recommend:

COCKTAIL There is a wide variety of cocktail glasses on the market, ranging anywhere from 3 to 6 ounces with varying sizes in between (such as $3\frac{1}{2}$, $4\frac{1}{2}$, $4\frac{3}{4}$, etc.). Again, personal taste will dictate, but, if possible, it's always nice to have two sizes (at least) on hand.

COLLINS Multiple-ingredient drinks are usually served in collins glasses, as are many "juice" and "cola" drinks. They range from 10 to about 14 ounces, and there are some, called tall collins, that can be as large as 16 ounces.

DOUBLE ROCKS (also called doubles) For "rocks" drinks, these range from 12 to 16 ounces.

GOBLET Again, there is a wide variety of goblets. Beer goblets are traditionally 12 ounces, whereas other types can range from 10 to 14 ounces.

Hurricane Glass Excellent for two-person exotic drinks, this huge goblet is usually 22 ounces. I have seen some in "Island" bars that were as big as 30 ounces!

Martini These V-shaped glasses, usually in the 4 to 5-ounce range, are perhaps the most famous of the lot.

OLD Fashioned (also called lowball or rocks). Very common glasses in the 6 to 8-ounce range. A double old fashioned holds 2 to 4 ounces more.

Don't let your glassware—or lack thereof—dictate the drink. Virtually any elixir can be served in any type of glass. The exceptions are those mammoth, two- and three-person, multi-ingredient concoctions. Otherwise, don't sweat it, just drink it!

Measurements

Here's a little chart to make sure all your pours are accurate:

1 cup	**8 ounces**
1 split	**6.4 ounces**
1 wineglass	**4 ounces**
1 jigger	**1½ ounces**
1 pony	**1 ounce**
1 tablespoon (tbsp.)	**⅜ ounce**
1 teaspoon (tsp.)	**⅛ ounce**
1 dash	**1/32 ounce**

Bottle Sizes of Wines & Spirits

When you do your shopping, these are the measurements you will encounter:

Type	Fluid ozs.	Metric equivalents
gallon	**128.0**	**3.5 l**
double magnum	**101.4**	**3.0 l**
half-gallon	**64.0**	**1.9 l**
magnum	**50.7**	**1.5 l**
quart	**32.0**	**1.0 l**
fifth	**25.6**	**750 ml**
pint	**16.0**	**460 ml**
tenth	**12.8**	**375 ml**
half-pint	**8.0**	**230 ml**
split	**6.4**	**187 ml**
miniature	**1.6**	**50 ml**

Mixers, Garnishes, and "Extras"

Stocking your Tiki Bar is a matter of personal taste, but here are the mainstays:

Bananas

Bitters—the two most popular varieties are orange and Angostura

Club soda, seltzer, tonic water

Cola, Sprite or 7-Up, ginger ale

Cream—light and heavy

Cream of coconut

Grenadine—made from pomegranates, this sweet, colorful (red) flavoring will see a lot of use

Ice—and plenty of it

Ice cream & sherbet

Juices—apple, cranberry, grapefruit, lemon, lime, orange, passion fruit, pineapple, prune, and tomato. Other "exotic" juices and nectars (kiwi, star fruit, mango, etc.) are available

Lemons, limes, oranges

Maraschino cherries

Milk

Mint leaves—used occasionally

Piña colada mix and sour mix—if caught short on fresh ingredients, these will do

Pineapple slices or spears

Rock candy syrup—can be substituted for sugar, or to add a touch of sweetness to any recipe

Rose's lime juice—differs from fresh lime juice because it contains a sugar-based syrup

Salt

Sugar—white granulated sugar and brown sugar are used most often

Sugar cane swizzle sticks—a nice touch for any exotic libation

Tiki umbrellas and other cute decorations you can find at party stores

Tiki Liquors

A well-stocked Tiki bar requires a fraction of the liquors needed for a traditional bar.

Amaretto—almond-flavored liqueur

Bailey's—Irish cream liqueur

Brandy—speaking Tiki, flavored brandies (banana, cherry, blackberry) are the most popular

Crème liqueurs—crème de cacao, crème de banana, and crème de menthe are worthy additions to any Tiki bar

Curaçao—both blue and orange

Gin—liquor distilled from rye and other grains and flavored with juniper berries

Kahlua—Mexican coffee-flavored liqueur

Rum—the most common ingredient in the vast majority of Tiki drinks. I'd suggest a five bottle set up, consisting of light rum, dark rum, gold rum, 151-proof rum, and one of the flavored rums, preferably coconut

Tia María—this Jamaican coffee-flavored liqueur is good to have on hand

Triple Sec—orange-flavored liqueur

Tequila—a must for margaritas

Vodka—one bottle should do the trick. Having a bottle of citrus-flavored vodka as well would be a good idea

Helpful Hints

Before you start pouring, here are a few helpful hints to enhance your mixology skills.

SHAKING AND STIRRING
You *stir* a drink, such as a martini, when you want to avoid cloudiness and bubbles. You *shake* a drink when you need to thoroughly combine ingredients for taste, consistency, and color. In Tiki land, you'll be using your cocktail shaker and strainer most of the time, so pay close attention to the recipe.

CHILLING THE GLASSES Unless otherwise specified, *always* chill a cocktail glass before serving a drink in it. This can be done by filling it with ice cubes while you mix the drink, filling it with ice water while you mix the drink, or refrigerating it for 30–60 minutes before using it. Chilling is especially important for piña coladas or any other Tiki drinks served in goblets, hurricanes, collins, or tall collins glasses.

FROSTING THE GLASSES To frost a glass with salt or sugar, use a lemon or lime wedge to moisten the rim of the glass; then dip the rim into a saucer filled with the salt or sugar. Be careful not to press too hard, especially with glasses that have a thin edge. To frost with ice, dip the rim of the glass in water, then place glass in a freezer for 30–45 minutes. For frosting beer mugs, dip the entire mug in water and freeze.

FLOATING A LIQUEUR or any other ingredient, atop a completed cocktail: slowly pour the ingredient to be 'floated' over the backside of a teaspoon or a fat swizzle stick. If you do it right, the 'floated' addition should remain at the top.

GARNISHING A DRINK Always add the garnish last.

Congratulations!

YOU'RE READY TO BEGIN MIXING.

ACAPULCO

1 ½ oz. rum
½ oz. triple sec
½ oz. lime juice

¼ tsp. sugar
1 egg white
1 mint leaf

Fill a cocktail shaker with ice, add ingredients, and shake well. Strain into an ice-filled old fashioned glass and garnish with mint leaf.

Agent Orange

¾ oz. vodka
½ oz. apple schnapps
½ oz. melon liqueur

2 tbsp. grenadine
4 oz. orange juice
3–4 oz. crushed ice

Blend all ingredients until smooth, pour into a chilled goblet or hurricane glass, and garnish with an orange slice.

ALOHA

1 oz. dark rum
1 oz. Myers's Rum Cream
  Liqueur
2 oz. orange juice
2 oz. pineapple juice
  (or 2 oz. pineapple chunks)

1 oz. coconut syrup
1 tbsp. lime juice
1 scoop vanilla ice cream
2–3 oz. crushed ice

Blend all ingredients until smooth, pour
into a chilled goblet or hurricane glass,
and garnish with a pineapple wedge.

17

Amaretto Sunset
(FROZEN)

1 oz. Amaretto
½ oz. dark rum
3 oz. orange juice
1 tsp. lemon juice
3–4 oz. crushed ice

Blend all ingredients (except
lemon juice) until smooth,
pour into a chilled goblet or
hurricane glass, and garnish
with a maraschino cherry.
Float the lemon juice.

AMBERJACK

1 ½ oz. applejack (apple brandy)
½ oz. light rum
2 oz. orange juice
1 oz. pineapple juice

Fill a cocktail shaker with ice, add ingredients, and shake well. Pour into a chilled collins glass and garnish with a maraschino cherry.

ATLANTIC BREEZE

¾ oz. light rum
¾ oz. apricot brandy
¾ oz. Galliano

4 oz. pineapple juice
1 oz. lemon juice
1 tsp. grenadine

Fill a cocktail shaker with ice, add all ingredients (except grenadine), and shake well. Strain into an ice-filled collins glass and garnish with a maraschino cherry and an orange slice. Float the grenadine.

BAHAMA MAMA

1 ½ oz. light rum **2 oz. pineapple juice**
1 ½ oz. gold rum **2 oz. orange juice**
1 ½ oz. dark rum **Dash grenadine***
2 oz. sour mix   **(optional)**

Fill a cocktail shaker with ice, add ingredients, and shake well. Pour into a chilled goblet, collins glass, or hurricane glass and garnish with two maraschino cherries, an orange slice, and a pineapple wedge.

*If using grenadine, add to the bottom of the serving glass before pouring.

FROZEN BAHAMA MAMA—Blend all ingredients (except grenadine) with 3–4 oz. of crushed ice until smooth. Pour into a chilled goblet or hurricane glass and garnish.

Banana Daiquiri
(FROZEN)

1–2 oz. light rum
1 oz. banana liqueur*
½ oz. lime juice

½ oz. cream
¼–½ banana
3–4 oz. crushed ice

Blend all ingredients until smooth, pour into a chilled goblet or hurricane glass, and garnish with an orange slice or maraschino cherry.

* For other flavors (strawberry, coconut, etc.), substitute appropriate liqueur for banana liqueur.

BIG BAMBOO LOVE SONG

2 oz. dark rum
1 oz. light rum
½ oz. triple sec
1 oz. orange juice

1 oz. pineapple juice
1 oz. lime juice
¾ oz. fruit syrup

Fill a cocktail shaker with ice, add ingredients, and shake well. Pour into a collins glass.

Courtesy—Couples Resort, Ocho Rios, Jamaica

Blue Marlin

1 shot blue Curaçao
1 shot light rum
4 oz. lemon-lime mix

Fill a cocktail shaker with ice, add ingredients, and shake well. Strain into a chilled martini glass.

Courtesy—Marlin Hotel, Miami Beach, Florida

BLUE SHARK

1 ½ oz. tequila
1 ½ oz. vodka
1 ½ oz. blue Curaçao

Fill a cocktail shaker with ice, add ingredients, and shake well. Strain into an ice-filled old fashioned glass.

BUCCANEER

1 ½ oz. Capt. Morgan's Spiced Rum
½ oz. Malibu rum
½ oz. Drambuie
½ oz. cream

Fill a cocktail shaker with ice, add ingredients, and shake well. Pour into an old fashioned glass.

CACTUS COLADA

2 oz. tequila
2 oz. cream of coconut
4 oz. pineapple juice

Blend all ingredients until smooth, pour into a chilled collins glass, and garnish with an orange slice and a maraschino cherry.

Caicos Cooler

1 ½ oz. rum
1 oz. Cointreau
½ oz. vodka
½ oz. banana liqueur
2 oz. orange juice

Fill a cocktail shaker with ice, add ingredients, and shake well. Pour into a cocktail glass and garnish with a maraschino cherry and a pineapple wedge.

CARIBBEAN HUMMER

1 oz. light rum
1 oz. dark rum
½ oz. Scotch
½ oz. pineapple juice
7-Up or Sprite

Fill a collins glass with ice, add all ingredients (except 7-Up), stir and fill with 7-Up. Garnish with a pineapple wedge.

Caribbean Sunset

¾ oz. rum
¾ oz. gin
¾ oz. blue Curaçao

¾ oz. banana liqueur
1 oz. lemon juice
1 oz. lime juice

Fill a cocktail shaker with ice, add ingredients, and shake well. Pour into a cocktail glass and garnish with a mint sprig and lime slice.

CASTAWAY

2 oz. dark rum
1 oz. banana liqueur
1 oz. cream of coconut

Fill a cocktail shaker with ice, add ingredients, and shake well. Strain into an ice-filled old fashioned glass.

CHI-CHI

1–2 oz. light rum
½ oz. blackberry brandy
4 oz. pineapple juice

Fill cocktail shaker with ice, add ingredients, and shake well. Pour into a chilled collins glass and garnish with a maraschino cherry and/or pineapple wedge.

CHOCOLADA

1 ½ oz. dark crème de cacao
1 oz. light rum
½ oz. white crème de cacao

1 oz. cream of coconut
1 oz. pineapple juice
1 tbsp. chocolate syrup
3 oz. crushed ice

Blend all ingredients (except chocolate syrup) until smooth and pour into a chilled goblet. Float the chocolate syrup.

Chocolate Black Russian

1 ½ oz. Kahlua
1 oz. vodka
1–2 scoops chocolate ice cream
3 oz. crushed ice (optional)

Blend all ingredients until smooth and pour into a chilled goblet.

COCONUT KISS

2 oz. Malibu rum
½ oz. Kahlua
3 oz. pineapple juice
3–4 oz. ice

Blend all ingredients (except Kahlua) until smooth. Pour into a chilled collins glass, float the Kahlua, and garnish with a maraschino cherry.

Courtesy—World Yacht Club, New York, New York

Deep Pacific

1 ½ oz. vodka
1 ½ oz. light rum
1 oz. blue Curaçao
1 tbsp. green Chartreuse
7-Up

Fill a collins glass with ice, add all ingredients (except 7-Up), stir, and fill with 7-Up.

FROZEN BIKINI

2 oz. vodka
1 oz. peach schnapps
**1 oz. champagne
 (chilled)**

2 oz. orange juice
3 oz. peach nectar
Splash of lemon juice
3–4 oz. crushed ice

Blend all ingredients (except champagne) until smooth, pour into a chilled goblet, and top with champagne.

FROZEN MARGARITA

1 ½ oz. tequila
½ oz. triple sec
1 oz. sour mix

1 to 2 dashes Rose's
 lime juice*
3–4 oz. crushed ice

Blend all ingredients until smooth and pour into a chilled, salt-rimmed goblet or margarita glass.

*Add various fruits and/or fruit syrups as desired.

GOING BANANAS

1–1 ½ oz. banana liqueur
½ oz. banana-flavored rum
 (or light rum)
½ oz. white crème de cacao

1 tsp. vanilla
1 scoop vanilla ice cream
½ banana
3 oz. crushed ice

Blend all ingredients until smooth, pour into a chilled goblet or hurricane glass, and float an extra teaspoon of banana rum or banana liqueur. Garnish with a banana slice.

Golden Colada

2 oz. Amaretto
1 oz. gold rum
2 oz. cream of coconut
2 oz. pineapple juice
3 oz. crushed ice

Blend all ingredients until smooth, pour into a chilled goblet or collins glass, and garnish with a maraschino cherry.

HAWAIIAN HIGHBALL

1 oz. vodka
4 oz. Trader Vic's Mai Tai Mix
Splash of soda

Fill a cocktail shaker with ice, add ingredients (except soda), and shake well. Pour into a collins glass and top with soda.

Hawaiian Orgasm

1 ½ oz. vodka
1 ½ oz. light rum
1 tbsp. green Chartreuse
1 tbsp. yellow Chartreuse

½ tsp. blue Curaçao
Equal parts pineapple &
  orange juice (2–4 oz. each

Fill a cocktail shaker with ice, add ingredients, and shake well. Strain into an ice-filled goblet and garnish with a maraschino cherry and pineapple wedge.

HONG KONG SUNDAE

1 oz. Galliano
½ oz. Cointreau
1 scoop orange sherbet

Blend all ingredients until smooth, pour into a chilled goblet, and garnish with a maraschino cherry.

HORNY MONKEY

1 ½ oz. banana liqueur
1 oz. vodka
½ oz. light rum
2 oz. cream of coconut

pineapple juice
1 banana, peeled
cinnamon

Fill a cocktail shaker with ice, add all ingredients (except pineapple juice), and shake well. Strain into an ice-filled collins glass, fill with pineapple juice, and garnish with a whole banana. Dust with cinnamon.

HOT SAND-SATION

1 oz. vodka
1 oz. Capt. Morgan's
    Spiced Rum
1 oz. light rum

3 oz. orange juice
½ oz. sour mix
3–4 oz. crushed ice
1 tsp. 151-proof rum

Blend all ingredients (except 151-proof rum) until smooth and pour into a chilled collins glass. Float the 151-proof rum and garnish with a maraschino cherry.

Hurricane Wind

2 oz. Malibu rum   or passion fruit
1 oz. Southern   juice
    Comfort   1 tbsp. lime juice
1 oz. mango nectar   1 tsp. grenadine

Fill a cocktail shaker with ice, add ingredients and shake well. Strain into an ice-filled old fashioned glass and garnish with a maraschino cherry.

ICEBALL

1 oz. gin
1 oz. white crème de menthe
½ oz. Sambuca
2 tbsp. cream
3–4 oz. crushed ice

Blend all ingredients until smooth and pour into a chilled goblet or hurricane glass.
GREEN ICEBALL—Use green crème de menthe.

Island Coffee

1 oz. dark rum
1 oz. Kahlua
½ oz. cream
1 tsp. coffee liqueur
Iced coffee

Fill a goblet, collins, or hurricane glass with ice, add ingredients (except coffee liqueur) and fill with iced coffee. Stir, top with whipped cream, and drizzle the coffee liqueur.

FROZEN ISLAND COFFEE—Blend all ingredients (except coffee liqueur) with 3–4 oz. crushed ice until smooth and pour into a chilled goblet. Top with whipped cream and drizzle the coffee liqueur.

JAMAICAN ME KRAZY

1 oz. Jamaican rum
½ oz. coconut rum
½ oz. white crème de cacao
½ oz. banana liqueur

1 oz. cream
1 tsp. gold rum
3 oz. crushed ice

Blend all ingredients (except gold rum) until smooth, pour into a chilled goblet or hurricane glass, and float the gold rum.

KAHLUA HUMMER

1 oz. Kahlua
1 oz. light rum
1 scoop vanilla ice cream

Blend all ingredients until smooth, pour into a chilled goblet.

MALAYSIAN DREAM
(MALAYSIAN COLADA)

1 ½ oz. vodka
2 oz. cream of coconut
4 oz. pineapple juice
1 tsp. grenadine
3–4 oz. crushed ice

Blend all ingredients until smooth, pour into a chilled goblet or hurricane glass, and garnish with a maraschino cherry and a pineapple wedge.

Menehune Juice

2 oz. light rum
4 oz. Trader Vic's Mai Tai Mix
Juice of 1 fresh lime

Fill a cocktail shaker with ice, add ingredients, and shake well. Pour into a collins glass and garnish with a mint sprig and lime slice or wedge.

MIDORI COLADA
(A.K.A. MELON COLADA OR FROG COLADA)

¾ oz. Midori
1 ½ oz. light rum
1 oz. cream of coconut
3 oz. pineapple juice
2 tbsp. cream
2–3 pieces fresh honeydew
melon (sweet)
3–4 oz. crushed ice

Blend all ingredients until smooth, pour into a chilled goblet, collins, or hurricane glass, and garnish with a fresh melon ball. *FROG COLADA*—Float 1 tsp. of grenadine or cherry liqueur before garnishing.

Mudslide

1 oz. vodka
1 oz. Kahlua
1 oz. Bailey's Irish Cream

Fill a cocktail shaker with ice, add ingredients, and shake well. Strain into a chilled cocktail glass.
MUDSLIDE ON THE ROCKS—Fill a cocktail shaker with ice, add ingredients, and shake well. Pour into an old fashioned glass.
FROZEN MUDSLIDE—Blend all ingredients with 3–4 oz. of crushed ice until smooth and pour into a chilled goblet or hurricane glass.

PARADISE

1 oz. gin
1 oz. apricot brandy
1 ½ oz. orange juice

Fill a cocktail shaker with ice, add ingredients, and shake well. Strain into an ice-filled old fashioned glass.

PARADISE LOST

2 oz. vodka
1 oz. cherry brandy
2 oz. pineapple juice

Fill a cocktail shaker with ice, add ingredients, and shake well. Strain into an ice-filled old fashioned glass.

PASSION PUNCH

2 oz. gin
1 oz. brandy
12–16 oz. passion fruit juice
Juice of 1 lime
Dash of bitters

Fill a cocktail shaker with ice, add ingredients, and shake well. Pour into a large goblet or 2-person scorpion bowl and garnish with a fresh flower, preferably a gardenia.

Pensacola Bushwacker

1 oz. banana rum
1 oz. coconut rum
1 tsp. 151-proof rum
Equal parts orange & pineapple juice
   (1–3 oz. each)

Add all ingredients (except 151-proof rum) to an ice-filled collins or tall collins glass and stir. Float 151-proof rum and garnish with a maraschino cherry.

PIÑA COLADA

1 ½ oz. light rum   **2 oz. pineapple juice**
1 ½ oz. cream of coconut   **Splash of cream**
2 oz. pineapple chunks

Blend all ingredients until smooth, pour into a chilled collins glass, and garnish with a maraschino cherry and an orange slice.

FROZEN PIÑA COLADA—Blend all ingredients with 3–4 oz. of crushed ice until smooth, pour into a chilled goblet or hurricane glass, and garnish with a maraschino cherry and an orange slice.

Note: Numerous Piña Colada mixes are available.

Pinky Gonzales

1 ½ oz. tequila
4 oz. Trader Vic's Mai Tai Mix

Fill a cocktail shaker with ice, add ingredients, and shake well. Strain into an ice-filled collins glass and garnish with a mint sprig.

PIRATE COCKTAIL

1 ½ oz. Jamaican rum
½ oz. sweet vermouth
1–2 dashes Angostura bitters

Fill a cocktail shaker with ice, add ingredients, and shake well. Strain into an ice-filled cocktail or rocks glass.

PIRATE'S COVE

1 ½ oz. dark rum   **2 oz. pineapple juice**
1 ½ oz. light rum   **3 oz. cream of coconut**
½ oz. gold rum   **1 oz. crushed ice**

Blend all ingredients until smooth, pour into a chilled goblet.

Pirate's Grog

2 oz. light rum   **2 tbsp. grenadine**
1 oz. spiced rum   **1 tsp. lime juice**
2 tbsp. Amaretto   **1 tsp. lemon juice**

Fill a cocktail shaker with ice, add ingredients, and shake well. Strain into an ice-filled old fashioned glass and garnish with a lemon twist.

Planter's Punch

2 oz. Myer's dark rum   **1 tsp. sugar**
3 oz. orange juice   **Dash of grenadine**
Juice of ½ lemon or
   lime

Fill a cocktail shaker with ice, add ingredients, and shake well. Pour into a collins glass and garnish with a maraschino cherry.

PONCE DE LEON

2 oz. light rum
2 tbsp. mango nectar
2 tbsp. grapefruit juice
1 tsp. lemon juice

Fill a cocktail shaker with ice, add ingredients, and shake well. Strain into an ice-filled collins glass.

Rastafarian

2 oz. Jamaican rum
½ oz. gold rum
1 tsp. banana liqueur
1 ½ oz. cream of coconut
1 ½ oz. pineapple juice

Fill a cocktail shaker with ice, add ingredients, and shake well. Strain into an ice-filled old fashioned glass.

RUM JUNGLE

½ oz. light rum

½ oz. dark rum

½ oz. coconut rum

½ oz. Capt. Morgan's
  Spiced Rum

2 oz. pineapple juice

2 oz. orange juice

1 banana, peeled

3–4 oz. crushed ice

Blend all ingredients until smooth and pour into a chilled goblet. Garnish with a whole banana.

SAMOAN FOG CUTTER

2 oz. light rum

1 oz. brandy

½ oz. gin

½ oz. orgeat syrup

1 tsp. sweet sherry

2 oz. orange juice

2 oz. lemon juice

Fill a cocktail shaker with ice, add all ingredients (except sweet sherry), and shake well. Pour into a chilled goblet, float the sweet sherry, and garnish with a maraschino cherry.

SCORPION

2 oz. light rum (gold rum can be substituted)
1 oz. brandy
½ oz. crème de noyaux

2 oz. orange juice
½ oz. lemon juice
3–4 oz. crushed ice

Blend all ingredients until smooth and pour into a chilled goblet or hurricane glass. Garnish with an orange slice.

For 2—double all ingredients except rum; use 5 oz.

Sea Breeze

1 ½ oz. vodka
2 oz. grapefruit juice
3 oz. cranberry juice

Fill a collins glass with ice, add ingredients, and stir.

SEX ON THE BEACH

¾ oz. vodka
¾ oz. peach schnapps
Equal parts cranberry & pineapple juice
(1–3 oz. each)

Fill a collins glass with ice, add vodka and peach schnapps, then fill with juice and stir. Garnish with a maraschino cherry (optional).

SEX ON A FROZEN BEACH—Blend all above ingredients plus ½ oz. of blue Curaçao with 3 oz. of crushed ice until smooth. Pour into a chilled goblet and garnish with two maraschino cherries.

58

Singapore Sling

1 oz. gin   **Dash of cherry brandy**
2 oz. sour mix   **Club soda**
½–¾ oz. grenadine

Fill a cocktail shaker with ice, add all ingredients (except club soda & cherry brandy), and shake well. Strain into an ice-filled collins glass, fill with club soda, and float the cherry brandy.

SLIPPERY MONKEY

¾ oz. vodka

¾ oz. coconut rum

¾ oz. coffee liqueur

¾ oz. crème de banana

1 scoop vanilla ice cream

3 oz. crushed ice

Blend all ingredients until smooth, pour into a chilled hurricane glass, and garnish with a maraschino cherry.

Courtesy—Churchill's Attic, St. Augustine, Florida

STINGER

(FROZEN)

1 ½ oz. brandy

½ oz. white crème de menthe

½ scoop vanilla ice cream (optional)

3 oz. crushed ice

Blend all ingredients until smooth, pour into a chilled goblet, and garnish with a maraschino cherry.

strawberry blonde

1 oz. gold rum
¾ oz. crème de noyaux
½ oz. crème de cacao
1–2 scoops vanilla ice
  cream

4 or 5 whole strawberries
  without stems
1 tbsp. strawberry liqueur
2 oz. crushed ice (optional)
Whipped cream

Blend all ingredients (except strawberry liqueur and whipped cream) until smooth and pour into a chilled goblet. Top with whipped cream and drizzle the strawberry liqueur.

Submariner

2 oz. vodka
1 ½ oz. light rum
1 ½ oz. spiced rum
1 tbsp. melon liqueur
1 tsp. lemon juice

Fill a cocktail shaker with ice, add ingredients, and shake well. Strain into an ice-filled old fashioned glass and garnish with a twist of lime.

SUFFERING BASTARD

1 ½ oz. light rum
1 ½ oz. dark rum
1 tbsp. Curaçao
¼–½ tsp. sugar
Juice of 1 lime

Fill a cocktail shaker with ice, add ingredients, and shake
well. Strain into an ice-filled old fashioned glass, add
lime halves, and garnish with cucumber peel.

Tequila Sunrise

1 ½ oz. tequila
½ oz. grenadine
½ tsp. lime juice
Orange juice

Fill a collins glass with ice, add tequila and
lime juice, fill with orange juice, and stir.
Insert swizzle stick into the glass and pour
the grenadine down the stick, enabling it to
reach the bottom and "rise."

TIKI MAI TAI

1 ½ oz. rum
1 oz. crème de noyaux
¾ oz. triple sec

1 oz. pineapple juice
1 oz. sweet & sour mix
3 oz. crushed ice

Blend all ingredients until smooth and pour into a chilled collins or hurricane glass.

Courtesy—Sea World's Polynesian Luau, Orlando, Florida

T.I. SPECIAL

½ oz. Amaretto
¼ oz. coconut rum
¼ oz. cherry brandy

¼ oz. peach schnapps
Splash of pineapple juice
Splash of 7-Up

Fill a cocktail shaker with ice, add ingredients, and shake well. Pour into a cocktail glass and garnish with an orange slice.

Courtesy—Treasure Island Inn, Daytona Beach Shores, Florida

VIEQUENSE

2 oz. rum
1 oz. Amaretto
2 oz. orange juice
2 oz. Coco Lopez

Fill a cocktail shaker with ice, add ingredients, and shake well. Pour into a hurricane glass and garnish with a maraschino cherry and an orange slice.

Courtesy—Bananas Resort, Vieques, Puerto Rico

Voodoo
(FROZEN)

2 oz. dark rum
1 oz. light rum
1 tbsp. vodka
1 tbsp. whiskey

2 oz. pineapple juice
2 oz. orange juice
3–4 oz. crushed ice

Blend all ingredients until smooth, pour into a chilled goblet or hurricane glass, and garnish with a lemon slice.

WHITE SHARK

2 oz. light rum
1 oz. vodka
1 oz. Sambuca
2 oz. cream of coconut

1–2 scoops vanilla ice cream
2–3 oz. crushed ice

Blend all ingredients until smooth, pour into a chilled goblet or hurricane glass, and dust with coconut shavings.

Zombie

1 oz. light rum
¾ oz. crème de noyaux
½ oz. triple sec
1 ½ oz. sour mix

1 ½–2 oz. orange juice
1 tbsp. 151-proof rum
3–4 oz. crushed ice

Blend all ingredients (except 151-proof rum) until smooth, pour into a chilled goblet or hurricane glass, float 151-proof rum, and garnish with a maraschino cherry.